THE
Archive Photographs
SERIES

BYERMOOR
MARLEY HILL
AND SUNNISIDE

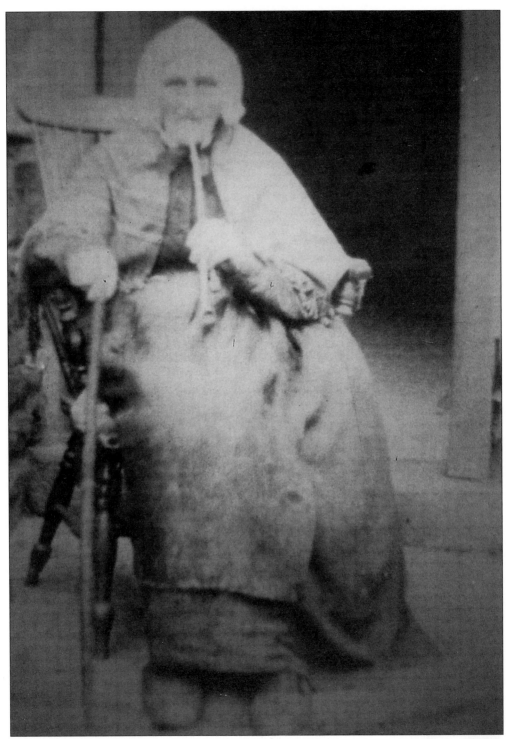

Elizabeth Smith, born 1782 and died 28 May 1884, aged 102 years. She married Thomas Smith, who was born 1763, and they became farmers at Crookgate. He died 24 March 1854, aged 91 years. Their family continued to farm at Crookgate for 200 years.

THE
Archive Photographs
SERIES

BYERMOOR MARLEY HILL AND SUNNISIDE

Compiled by
F.G. Newman and the
Sunniside and District Local History Society

CHALFORD

First published 1997
Copyright © F.G. Newman and the
Sunniside and District Local History Society, 1997

The Chalford Publishing Company
St Mary's Mill, Chalford,
Stroud, Gloucestershire, GL6 8NX

ISBN 0 7524 1046 6

Typesetting and origination by
The Chalford Publishing Company
Printed in Great Britain by
Bailey Print, Dursley, Gloucestershire

The Hobson Colliery (later renamed Burnopfield) with coal chaldrons in the foreground, 1900. The colliery was owned in the mid 1800s by John Berkley of Newcastle. In 1849 Bowes and Partners took it over. The colliery stood across the valley to the west of Byermoor and closed in July 1968.

Contents

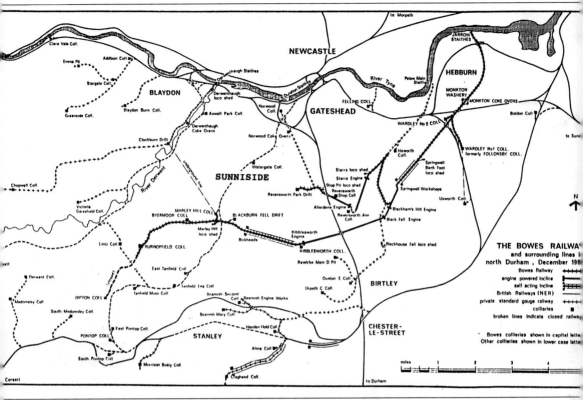

The Bowes Railway & Surrounding Lines, 1965. At the time this map was printed the coal mining industry was already in decline. There were 42 collieries, 3 drifts, 4 staithes, 3 cokeworks, 6 loco sheds, 1 workshop and 1 engine works spread across the region. None of them have survived.

Introduction

On Tuesday 3 March 1992 at 7.30 pm, a group of enthusiasts met at Sunniside Workingmen's Social Club to discuss the possibility of forming a local history society. It was resolved by all present that the Sunniside and District Local History Society be formed. An election took place and the following were elected: Chairman: Mr F.G. Newman, Secretary: Mrs E. Batey, Treasurer: Mrs S. Gascoigne, Assistant Chairman: Mr E. Hayden, Assistant Secretary: Ms M. Debie. Other founder members present were: Christine Casey, Peter Davison, Jean Mackie, Jack Morton, Margaret Newman and Ken Williams.

Over the years the interest shown has exceeded all of our expectations and to date we have in excess of 120 members, many of whom now live outside the area but still attend meetings each month, even in the worst winter weather. Their unstinting enthusiasm has never waned. It is thanks to the continued support of those members that we are able to produce this pictorial history of Byermoor, Marley Hill, Sunniside and the surrounding areas.

We are certain that this book will be of great interest to everyone in the community. To be reminded of loved ones and friends long gone, to see again streets and buildings long forgotten, will, we hope, be a source of great pleasure and revive many happy memories. We also hope that this, the very first authorised publication of the Society, will create a renewed interest in our local history.

Our community was founded on the coal mining industry. Families came from across the British Isles, and to a lesser degree Europe, and they all had one object in common, seeking work. It is a unique community; three separate villages, who through work, marriage and friendship, are now to their great credit fully integrated.

The coal mines have gone but the community spirit lives on. It is to the people past and present of Byermoor, Marley Hill, Sunniside and the surrounding area, that we dedicate this book.

Acknowledgements

The compilers wish to thank the Society members who have worked so hard in researching their chosen subjects; Mrs Ethel Baker: Dunston Staithes, Mrs Mary Harrison: Memories of Old Sunniside, Mrs Edna Ibbetson: The Causey, Mrs Jean Mackie: Marley Hill church, Miss Sheila McGahon: Byermoor, Mr Raymond Spellman: Sunniside, Mrs Joan Telford: Marley Hill and the White Elephant Schools. We would also like to thank the Society members and members of the community who have provided for copy their precious photographs and old postcards. Margaret Newman for transferring all text on to computer disc and for proof reading. Mr John Caffrey for keeping our computer up and running. Mr Eddie Liddle of Midhurst in West Sussex for allowing us to copy his fathers photographs and handwritten autobiography. Sunniside Social Club Officials and Committee for providing our excellent meeting facilities completely free of charge and Club Steward Mr Alan Gleghorn for his valued assistance. The Northern Clubs Federation Brewery at Dunston for lending us valuable equipment in our early days and for providing prizes so generously during our fund raising efforts. Chalford Publishing North East Editor Andrew Clark for his guidance and his patience. Denise, Eileen and the girls, at Boots Photographic Department, the Gateshead Metro Centre.

Mrs Elizabeth Ratcliffe and her daughter 'Nellie', residents of the Hobson. It was a small community with most of the houses relatively close to the pit. The residents were subject to high levels of dust and noise twenty-four hours a day.

One

The Hobson to Byermoor

The village of Byermoor lies about one mile west of Marley Hill, where coal mining has been carried out for hundreds of years. Byermoor is of ancient origin and is mentioned in the Boldon Book (1183). It is recorded as Biermore or Beechemoor, meaning the bare moors.

The lands of Biermore, or Byermoor, were owned by a John De-Guildeford (1385) and then passed to his son John in 1429, when it is described as Biermore Juxta-Morley. Morley being the family name of the De-Marleys who resided at Gibside Hall and Marley Hill. Records at that time state that the lands contained eighty acres of arable, five of meadow, forty of moor and ten of woodland. In 1474 Joan De-Guildeford, heiress to the estates, married Thomas Hodgeson. The Hodgesons were an old established family in the area, wealthy landowners and well established in the coal industry. They had one son, also named Thomas, and in her Will and Letters of Instruction, Joan passed the ownership of the Byermoor Estates to her son, which now became the property of the Hodgesons. Shortly afterwards the father Thomas died and his widow Joan eventually remarried a member of the Robson family. The lands were then successively held by first Thomas, Hugh and then George Hodgeson. In 1556 the estates descended to the co-heirs of Richard Hodgeson.

The whole tenure was reunited by purchase into the family of the Harrisons, of Byermoor and Bryan's Leap, Burnopfield. In 1617 William Harrison on his death seized of the Byermoor (meaning in Law, had possession of) a messuage (dwelling house with outbuildings and land) containing a hundred acres of arable, as many of meadow, twice as much pasture, forty acres of woodland and two hundred of moor. All this was left in his Will to his son and heir William. One of the descendants of William Harrison married into the family of the Hardings of Hollinside Hall, near Gibside. As a result of this marriage, the estates passed to the Harding family.

In the years between 1730, their property and estates (including Byermoor) were passed by foreclosure of mortgage into the hands of the Bowes family of Gibside. The Bowes family became linked with Gibside through marriage into the Blakiston family, the previous owners of Gibside in 1691. This family (Blakiston) had interests in the coal industry and the new owners, the Bowes family, continued in this work. Down the years the Bowes family became large, wealthy land-owners and owned many coal-fields and collieries, including Byermoor Colliery, having previously acquired (by purchase) the colliery and mineral rights from its owner, Sir Thomas Clavering. Descendants of the Bowes family married into the Strathmore and Lyons families, to become known as the Bowes-Lyons, the Earls of Strathmore. One of these descendants, John Bowes, who had been a member of a group of private coal-owners known as 'The Grand Alliance', broke away from this organisation, and in 1884, he and Charles M. Palmer formed the John Bowes & Partners Private Company, which operated twelve collieries including Byermoor Colliery.

Robert Ratcliffe (son of Elizabeth), born 8 September 1901, died 4 April 1961. He married Mary Kilkenny on 21 April 1928, and worked in both the Hobson and Byermoor Pits. During the Second World War he served as an auxiliary firemen in his spare time.

This level crossing was on the Crookgate/ Hobson bank. Coal from the Dipton Delight and Hobson Pits passed through these en-route to, first of all Jarrow, then in later years Dunston Staithes via Byermoor and Marley Hill Pits.

The inset, top left, of the postcard shows the Crookgate/Hobson bank level crossing with the village of Burnopfield in the valley below.

Burnopfield in the valley to the north of the Hobson. The Grand Cinema, on the corner to the left, was the main source of entertainment for many years prior to the coming of television. People young and old came from the surrounding villages, mainly on a Saturday night. There were the cheaper seats at the front affectionately known as the 'dog end', while the seats at the back were usually occupied by courting couples. Matty Baker walked up and down the aisles constantly flashing his torch and demanding 'silence'. The balcony was simply referred to as 'upstairs', it was the posh end. Sadly the cinema closed and through neglect fell into a state of dereliction. The allotments in the background were sold to property developers.

The junction of Crookgate with Fellside Road. Coal trucks can be seen in the middle ground being pulled by steam engine through the level crossing gates. The Pack Horse public house on the corner was once the centre of activity for most of the Byermoor men during the coal mining days. It was a small pub then and nothing fancy, but generally filled to capacity with coal miners who never tired of each others company.

Overlooking the valley from the Hobson bank top, Crookgate lies in the foreground below. The old colliery houses, built between 1865 and 1890, can be seen half way up Byermoor bank. The large manager's house, one of the few remaining buildings, is to the right. The houses when built were very spartan. They were slightly improved prior to the First World War but still left a lot to be desired. By 1969, with all of the residents rehoused, the colliery houses were demolished. At the top of the picture is Byermoor Sacred Heart church and to its right the school.

Byermoor bank in 1926. The buses (Daimler Big Bertha's and 1925 SOS) in convoy, stretching back as far as the eye can see, were going on the Consett schools' annual outing. To the left can be seen the gable end of a row of the old colliery houses. Behind the third bus, and to the left, is one of the few existing photographs of the old Mission, known locally as the 'Tin Church' because it was made of corrugated metal sheets. It was built through the fund raising efforts of the Mothers' Union for the parishioners of Marley Hill church who resided at Byermoor. It cost £200 to build and was opened on 10 October 1893 by Bishop Sandford. It eventually outlived its usefulness and fell into a state of disrepair, it was finally demolished in 1966. The Hobson Colliery and pit heap can be seen on the skyline.

Byermoor Colliery from the top of the pit heap. Colliery houses are visible to the right of the wheelhouse. Coal mining had taken place in Byermoor for hundreds of years and by the mid-nineteenth century John Bowes & Partners had sunk a new colliery. By 1894 the colliery was producing 500 tons of coal per day and fed 156 beehive coke ovens. These were closed prior to 1914. The colliery went on to expand and increase production over the years, giving employment to generations of men. Sadly, like hundreds of other coal mines, it fell victim to the highly questionable policy of the Government of the day and ceased production on 31 January 1968.

Byermoor Colliery yard. In the foreground is the old canteen and offices. In the background can be seen the large colliery manager's house and two streets of colliery houses accessed from Byermoor bank.

Byermoor Colliery shaft top and wheelhouse. Wooden pit props are stacked to the side, ready to be taken to the coal face and used as roof supports.

Underground miners at the coal face. Billy Ratcliffe, on the extreme left, was a Byermoor miner for many years before he left to work in a coal mine in the midlands.

The oldest known photograph of Byermoor Sacred Heart church. The foundation stone was laid on 12 September 1875 and the church was officially opened by Bishop Chadwick on 8 October 1876. During the Irish potato famine the population in the area was increased by the arrival of Irish immigrants. In 1869 Bishop Chadwick gave Father Patrick Thomas Mathews the task of having a church built for the forming of a parish. The architects were Dunn & Hansom who designed the church in the early English and Gothic style. The church stands on a hill overlooking the beautiful Derwent Valley, the Cheviot Hills can be seen in the distance.

The founder of Byermoor church, the Revd Father Patrick Thomas Mathews, 1869-79. In 1867, as a travelling mission priest, he was appointed to found a mission at Sacriston, near Durham City. He remained there for two years and during that time he used to travel on horseback to Stanley to say Mass, then travel on to Burnopfield to say Mass in a house which belonged to a Doctor Grensill. The house originally stood opposite the Sun Inn public house, but was demolished many years ago. When Father Mathews was appointed to oversee the building of Byermoor church he was residing at Lintz Green, Burnopfield. A wooden building served as the first church until 1871, it stood on the hillside where Crookgate garage now stands. Father Mathews faced many problems which must have seemed formidable but he eventually succeeded in having the church built. After ten years of service as parish priest at Byermoor, Father Mathews was appointed to St Joseph's parish at Gateshead.

The Very Revd Canon John Wilson, 1879-1914. After Father Mathews left the parish, Father John Wilson succeeded him in June 1879. He resided at Lintz Green for three years until 1882 when he was responsible for having the presbytery built adjoining the church. The Marquis of Bute paid half the cost and a large donation was made by Miss Surtees. Father Wilson was also responsible for installing benches in the church, for the design of the church grounds and, in 1883, for having a new school built. He took a great interest in a French association named 'Euvre Expiatoire' (Work of Expiation). For many years he was director of the English branch, translating many works into English. For this work he was appointed as Honorary Canon of the church of St Maria Sancto, Rome and a Knight of Malta. Canon Wilson died at Byermoor on 15 October 1914, aged 68 years.

A view of the church and presbytery from the south. The surrounding area has greatly changed since this picture was taken in the very early 1900s.

The church and presbytery viewed from Byermoor bank. The road was just a dirt track in these times, the late 1800s. The building is now partially obscured by trees.

The Revd Father Alfred Chadwick, 1914-25, was appointed parish priest a month after the death of Canon Wilson on 14 November 1914. He kept a diary in which he recorded daily events in the life of the parish. He recorded the many processions which took place during the months of May and June. In April 1915 the parishioners of Tantobie were transferred from Byermoor parish to Dipton parish and later in October 1918 the parishioners of Rowlands Gill were transferred from Byermoor parish to Chopwell parish. On 1 November 1918 new boundaries were then established. On 2 February 1925 Father Chadwick was transferred to Alnwick parish.

The interior of the church, when the only means of lighting was the huge oil lamp hanging over the centre of the aisle.

Canon Wilson in the church grounds.

The Revd Father Austin Pickering, 1925-68, the longest serving Byermoor priest to date.

The beautiful High Altar made from French Caen stone.

Kathleen Kilkenny, the first May Queen of Byermoor, c. 1928.

Father Pickering (centre), with missionary priests in the grounds of Byermoor church.

The opening of the Byermoor parish hall on 27 September 1930 by Bishop Thorman. It was used for all manner of functions including dances, wedding receptions, concerts and, for a period of ten years, a dining hall for the school children. Over the years it fell into disrepair and was demolished in May 1995.

A June Procession in 1943, depicting the Passion of Christ. Rear row, left to right: Sylvia Murray, Mary O'Brien, Rose Dwyer, Bernadette Walsh, Joan Hearne, Peggy Snaith. Front row: Mary Brough, Sheila McGahon, Dorothy Sewell, Moya O'Keefe, Lucy Reilly.

The Very Revd Canon Laurence Hollis at the wedding of Karen Newman to John Caffrey, in the gardens to the rear of the church, 21 June 1986. Father Hollis was appointed parish priest in May 1968. He was a former vice president of Ushaw College and had been in charge of music and the choir. Father Hollis was a member of the National Liturgical Commission and for eight years he served on the International Commission for English in the Liturgy (ICEL). He was appointed a Canon of the Diocese in February 1984. At Easter 1991, Canon Hollis became ill and spent several months away from the parish in convalescence. Unfortunately he was never well enough to return. He retired in March 1992 and died on 17 March 1997. He was a very popular priest and a sad loss to the community.

The Revd Father Andrew Faley, 1992-95.

The Revd Father John Taggart, 1995 - to date.

The Sacred Heart Parish School, Byermoor. Father John Wilson organised fund raising to build the present school and the Marquis of Bute gave a generous donation to the fund. Work commenced on the building of the new school in 1881 and on 5 January 1883 it was officially opened. It consisted of two classrooms and one large room. It was extended by one extra classroom in 1902. Electricity was installed in July 1963 and the school was extended in 1970, thanks to the efforts of Canon Hollis. In 1973 the school was again extended to include a kitchen and in 1982, gas central heating was installed. The school has survived threats of closure twice.

A Byermoor school class at the entrance of Byermoor church in the early 1900s, with Mr Nicholas Kelly, the headmaster from 1898-1912.

The school interior with the traditional
headmaster's stool standing next to the statue.
The stool is reputed to have been in existence
since the opening of the school.

Mr Daniel Henry, headmaster from 1912-26.

The school football team with Mr Matthew White.

A school class with Mr Matthew White, headmaster from 1926-37.

A school class, *c.* 1948, with Mr James Kehoe, headmaster from 1945-58.

A class play, *c.* 1946.

A school class, *c.* 1948.

A school play, c. 1951.

A school group, c. 1953.

Pupils of Byermoor School dressed for a play, c. 1953.

Left: Henry Gardner, headmaster from 1958-82. Right: Miss Mary Kim Bradley, born 10 April 1958, acting headteacher from 1992-94. She was herself a pupil at Byermoor School from 1962-72 and returned to become a teacher in 1981. She eventually became deputy head, serving under Anthony Hannon, and following his untimely retirement, Kim was appointed acting headteacher.

William Kilkenny, an Irish immigrant born 10 March 1876, who lived at Loughrae, County Galway. During the so called 'troubles' in Ireland and fearful that he would become involved, his uncle, who was a Bishop, arranged for him to go to England as coachman and gardener to Father Wilson of Byermoor. Here he met Anne Costello, whom he married in 1903. He then went to work for Mr Pickering, the colliery manager, as his gardener. He eventually went to work at the colliery in the boilerhouse and was allocated a colliery house at No. 17, Byermoor. He lived there until his death around 1932.

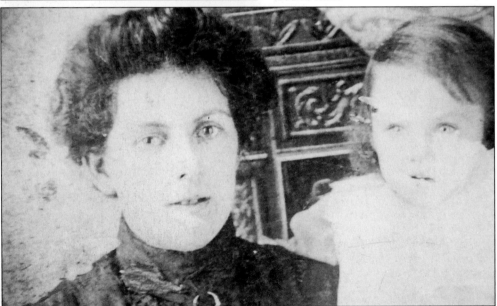

Anne Costello, born 13 May 1883 at Burnhope. Her father owned a barbers shop and also ran string and brass bands. They played at the opening of Byermoor church in 1876. She left school and went to work for Father Thompson at Stanley St Joseph's church. Father Wilson invited her to go to Byermoor as cook/housekeeper where she met William Kilkenny. They were married by Father Thompson at Stanley St Joseph's, and lived at first in one of the school houses at Byermoor. They had five children, Mary (pictured with her), Margaret, Winifred, Kathleen and William.

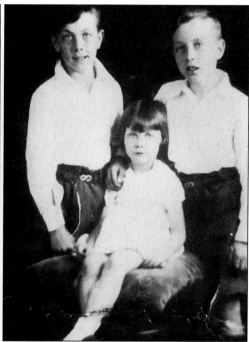

Mary Costello Kilkenny, 8 May 1904 to 27 August 1996, lived at Byermoor most of her life. She married Bob Ratcliffe, who died in 1961, and some years later she married Zanis Neilands who had originated from Latvia. In 1991, at the age of 86 years, and following the death of her second husband, she moved to Sun Hill, Sunniside. She died at Whickham Villa Nursing Home aged 92 years.

Billy Ratcliffe (left), 26 August 1928 to 23 August 1989, with his brother Austin, 23 July 1930 to 13 April 1997, and their sister Kathleen, born 26 July 1934. They were the children of Mary (nee Kilkenny) and Robert Ratcliffe.

Anne Kilkenny, c. 1930, by now residing at Byermoor. She was an unpaid midwife and nurse, treating patients referred to her by the local doctor. She would walk as far as Burnopfield, the Lintz, Barcus Close, Crookgate, High Row and Andrews Houses to deliver babies, sometimes in the middle of the night or in a blizzard. She was in big demand to make and ice, Christening, Christmas and wedding cakes, even when in her sixties. In 1938, following her husband's death, she very bravely moved to London. She stayed with friends until she found a house for herself and her children Kathleen and William. She took in boarders to earn a living then returned to the North East around 1950. For a short time she lived in Newcastle then moved back to Byermoor to live with her daughter Mary. She lived there until her death on 3 January 1965.

The Byermoor Exiles football team in 1910, so called because they were Irish immigrants.

The Byermoor Exiles in 1910.

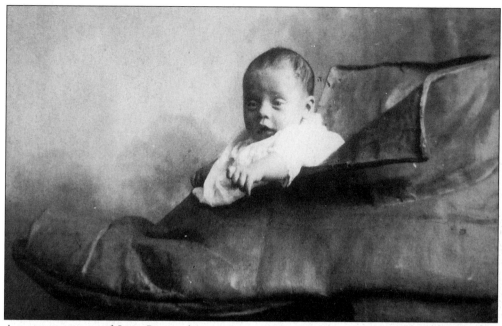

A unique picture of Jean Porter, born 3 June 1927. She was to marry Sunniside-born Les Eltringham.

William Ratcliffe of Byermoor and Mary Greener of South Stanley, signing the register at their wedding on 30 July 1955 in Byermoor Church, watched by Father Austin Pickering.

Arthur and Jenny Walker of Byermoor, on their wedding day in the 1920s.

The wedding of Magdalen Kilkenny and Andrew Graham at Byermoor church on 12 May 1943.

The Bell family wedding at Strathmore Crescent, Byermoor in the 1920s.

Two

In and Around Marley Hill

The name Marley Hill is derived from the de Merley family. In 1200 A.D. Adam de Merley was reported as being a witness to a charter of Walter de Urpeth. In the mid 1300s Ranulph owned the Manor, Gibside and Merley, being wholly agricultural, held in homage, fealty and one mark exchequer rent. He was a direct descendant of the de Merleys of Morpeth who owned land in other parts of Durham and Yorkshire. In 1534 Elizabeth Marley, only child and heiress of Richard de Marley, was contracted to Richard Blakeston, son of William Blakeston of Coxhoe. The marriage took place in 1539 and the ownership of the Marley Hill and Gibside property passed to the Blakeston family. By the seventeenth century the Marleys were yeoman at Urpeth and Picktree, the most famous of whom was Sir John Marley who had defended Newcastle with the Royalists during the 1642-51 Civil War.

A branch of the Hall family lived at Marley Hill early in the sixteenth century. They also held Crookgate, which was described as less than 50 acres, early in the seventeenth century. Coal had been wrought in the area from as early as 1402 and, in 1657, Sir William Blakiston granted a lease to William Carr of Newcastle to mine for coal at Northbanks and Marley Hill. In 1692 Sir Francis Blakiston granted a lease to Charles Montague for the right to mine coal at Gibside and Marley Hill. He was also given the right to lead coal over the Blakiston lands to the River Tyne, the lease to run out in 1722. In 1620 there were several small mines at work, and in 1752 there were three mines and a considerable village on Tinkler Fell. By 1760 Marley Hill Colliery was working to a depth of 36 fathoms and in the hands of John Bowes and Partners - The Grand Alliance. By 1815 they had abandoned the pit as unprofitable, to be re-opened in 1840 by John Bowes. Andrews House Colliery to the south of Marley Hill, but in close proximity, commenced production in 1843.

The Marley Hill Parish was formed by an order dated 6 August 1874. It included Marley Hill, Andrews House and Byermoor Collieries, the hamlets of Crookgate, Sunniside, Tinkler Fell and Streetgate as far as Watergate Bridge in Ravensworth, and also part of Fellside. The area was about 2,600 acres and the population was 2,912 by 1891. In the mid 1800s, with Marley Hill Pit producing well, three rows of back to back houses were built within yards of the shaft. They were known as Colliery Houses. In 1900 house building by John Bowes and Partners began for miners and their families in Marley Hill, these became known as New Houses. They were built on each side of the main road from Sunniside and consisted of four large houses for the colliery manager and other officials. Glamis Terrace was so named because John Bowes was a member of the Bowes-Lyons family whose seat was Glamis Castle. Church Street was where the church is situated and Cuthbert Street was also named after the church. After the Second World War 'pre-fab' houses were built at the west end of Marley Hill.

High Marley Hill in the 1920s, with a car struggling through mountainous snow drifts, so typical of those days.

"Peace" Bonfire 32'6" High
Marley Hill 19/7/19

The peace bonfire of 19 July 1919, built to celebrate the end of the First World War. Most of the timber came from the pits. The men carried and dragged old timber from as far away as Old Marley Hill and Byermoor Pits. There were other bonfires of celebration at High Marley Hill. In 1911 a huge one was built for the Coronation of George V and in May 1935 a bonfire was built to celebrate his Silver Jubilee. On each occasion unwanted materials from the mines and railways were dragged to the site and piled as high as thirty feet. The blaze could be seen many miles around, especially to the east.

The early diggings of High Marley Hill Drift, *c.* 1948.

High Marley Hill Drift in operation. It closed around 1963.

High Marley Hill School. It was built by Spoor of Whickham in May 1875 and the land donated by John Bowes. By the late 1950s attendance had dropped dramatically due to local people being housed elsewhere. The school closed in 1960, to be taken over by a wholesaler in 1961.

A class from High Marley Hill School, *c.* 1900.

A teacher outside the master's house at High Marley Hill School.

A class from High Marley Hill School, *c.* 1900.

Blackburn Fell Drift, about one mile to the south of Old Marley Hill, was opened in 1937 and employed approximately 200 men. The screens stood at the side of the Bowes Railway between Andrews Houses and Birkheads. The Marley Hill Coke Works had closed in that year, so many of those men found much needed work at the drift. During the working of the Brass Thill coal seams, evidence of previous digging was unearthed. The drift was self sufficient; it employed its own fitters and joiners, there was an electrician's shop and unlike the deep mine, where the ponies were kept underground, there was a stable on the surface for the ponies. The drift closed in 1978, the hewers, putters and other men working there were transferred to the nearby Marley Hill Pit.

Blackburn Fell Drift workers and ponies. Left to right: John Brown, H. Purvis, G. Parkin, P. Cohen (under manager).

Blackburn Fell Drift gate and entrance.

Pony drivers and hewers sharing their food with the ponies at Blackburn Fell Drift.

Blackburn Fell Drift staff at a presentation for winning coal mining's best kept and tidiest surface award in a regional competition in 1960.

Bob Gins, the Causey. The name Causey probably derived from the Roman Calcetum, meaning causeway. Prior to 1268, the Lords de la Leigh were Lords of the Manor. Around 1309, Joan de Charron married Bertram Monboucher and that family held the lands for about 100 years. The lands changed hands several times over the years, eventually becoming the property of the Shaftos in the 1900s. There were five houses at Bob Gins by the late 1700s. An 1857 map shows Causey Row, Causey Old Row, Causey New Row, Bob Gins and a public house.

A different angle, and a closer view, of the houses at Bob Gins.

The Causey School, or British School as it was first named. It was opened in 1866 in a few rooms in Causey Row. By 1870 it was numbered among those on the Grant List. The school building pictured was opened on 28 June 1897. The first headmaster was Mr E. Holden, there were five teachers and 150 pupils. Because of dwindling numbers of pupils the school closed in 1959. The last headmaster was Mr John Atkinson.

The Causey School headteacher John Atkinson with, on the right, caretaker Mrs Rhona Thompson (the mother of Edna Ibbetson who wrote the History of the Causey) and pupils.

The Causey Arch in the late 1800s. Sometimes called Tanfield or Dawson's Bridge, it was built by Wortley and Liddell to carry the famous Tanfield Waggonway, from Thomas Dawson's Causey and Tanfield Collieries over Causey Burn. The line became operational in July 1725 but this bridge collapsed. A second bridge was started in August 1725 and took more than a year to erect, it opened in 1727. Ralph Wood, a mason, built the first bridge and started the second, he was replaced in 1726 by H. Boag (1696-1763). The bridge has a span of 105ft, stands 80ft above the stream and is 22ft 7.5in wide. The arch is unique in that it has no central keystone. Its building costs, £2,252 16s 1d, were shared between Bowes, Liddell and Wortley.

The 'Causey Dykes' football team in the early 1900s.

In the late 1800s a Good Templars Lodge was formed at the Causey Chapel. These are members of the Lodge in the early 1900s.

High Row, formerly named Waggonway Row, built in the 1840s across two fields, known as Little and Taylor Close. At one time the houses at the east end were known as Low Row but eventually they all became known as High Row. They were demolished in 1960.

The front of High Row in March 1959, prior to demolition.

A rear view of High Row in March 1959 showing the allotments.

This photograph illustrates just how close the houses of High Row were to the railway line, the houses can be seen in the top left hand corner. The noise and dirt must have been a great nuisance and the closeness of the line a constant source of danger, especially to children.

Edward (Eddie) Liddle, born 14 February 1907. He wrote a diary depicting life at High Row. His very detailed description of the conditions in those days, his time at Marley Hill School and his years as a pony driver at Marley Hill Colliery are an important addition to local history archives. At the age of fourteen he described his first descent down the pit shaft: 'The cage seemed to drop away ever so fast and scared the life out of me, we were soon into the darkness and lost any sense of speed, this was a most strange feeling.' Eddie acknowledged from that day on that he was not cut out to be a miner. In truth his forte was writing but, like so many children in those days, it was expected that he would go down the pit and contribute to the family income. He went on to serve in the Middle East during the Second World War and eventually left the region. Eddie died on the 25 July 1982.

Marley Hill Spankers football team, formed 1926. They were formed to raise funds for needy children but entered the Birtley & District League and actually won one year.

Near the loco sheds, and to the south of Marley Hill Colliery, fourteen houses were completed by 1871 and named Bowes Terrace. Gibraltar Row, with fifteen houses, was built in 1874, followed some time later by seventeen houses named Marley Hill Terrace. They were collectively referred to as 'Andrews Houses', so named because of the land they stood on and the nearby colliery. This picture illustrates how close they were to the Bowes Railway line.

The Andrews Houses 'peace tea' held at Bowes Terrace in 1919, following the end of the First World War. The lady in the centre is Mrs Crosson and third from the right is her daughter-in-law Isobel Crosson.

Marley Hill Hole (The Valley). There were nineteen houses built in the mid 1840s, with very basic amenities, down in the low ground along the pit road past Sandygate. The street was originally known as Fen House Row but eventually became known as simply 'The Valley'. A mudslide carried away part of the street in the early 1900s and in 1920 they were demolished.

Mrs Anne King (nee Mahon) ran a shop from her house in The Valley c. 1900. Her husband Thomas was Scottish and she had two brothers, John and Michael. Anne had fifteen children but only twelve survived, seven girls and five boys. When married the daughters names were, Hannah Wilkie, Elizabeth McWorthers, Catherine Brown, Mary Brown (the Great Great Grandmother of Sunniside Dental Nurse Anne Kemp), Rosie Greener, Annie Harm, Susie Mordue. The sons were, Hugh, Tom, Paddy, Benny and Charles. Following the death of her husband, Anne would live with her daughters for six months at a time. She died aged 84 years on 14 February, year unknown. Charles died 1997 aged 89 years, the last survivor of her children.

Old Marley Hill viewed from the west. To the left can be seen the second Wesleyan chapel. It was built in 1870 on a plot of land donated by Bowes and Partners, at a cost of £350, and was eventually demolished in 1940. The three rows of colliery houses were built to the west of the colliery, in very close proximity. The left hand street was Front Row, the centre was quite simply Middle Row and, to the right, Coke Row or Cinderburners Row. The beehive coke ovens ran parallel with Coke Row in the valley below, hence the names, either of which would have been appropriate.

In 1853 a Primitive Methodist chapel was built on to the west end of Front Row. The street then became known as Chapel Row or, as some named it, 'Ranters Row'. In 1892 water mains were connected to the houses and gas mains were connected in 1914.

By March 1959 only Middle Row remained. The other two streets had been demolished in 1936, as the miners and their families were rehoused at Marley Hill council houses. Nellie Davidson (nee Aimers), who was born at Middlesbrough in 1902, came to Marley Hill with her father John William Aimers and the rest of her family because he was required to work in the new German Ovens. Nellie described in graphic detail the deplorable conditions they existed in. There was one room downstairs and one room upstairs accessed by an ordinary ladder. A single cold water tap stood in the room next to the window. The floor was uneven concrete and the rooms were always cold. The toilets were outside on rough ground and rats were very much in evidence both outside and inside the houses. The noise and dust from the colliery and railway lines were a hazard endured for twenty-four hours a day, seven days a week. Middle Row was eventually demolished in 1960.

Colliery pony drivers in 1912: Billy Storey, Billy Musgrove, Barty Casson, Billy Slater Bell, Billy Ellis, Alfy Blackmore, Billy Davison, Locky Wilkinson, Ralphy Bell, Tommy Davison, Jackie Storey.

The 'German Ovens', viewed from the south, Andrews House. Beehive coke ovens had been in use at Marley Hill Colliery since 1843. By the early 1900s they were considered to be in poor shape and had outlived their usefulness. In 1907 a batch of sixty Hussener by-product ovens were installed to the west of the colliery by the Coal Distillation Co. of Middlesbrough. These were built on the high ground above the now closed beehive ovens. When new coke works were opened at Monkton in 1937, the Marley Hill German Ovens were deemed obsolete and closed in that same year.

A closer view of the German Ovens showing the men at work.

During the First World War most of the men had been called up for military service and the ladies pictured were employed to replace some of them at the cokeworks. Nellie Aimers, seen here in the light coloured coat sitting third from the left, acted as messenger. She delivered letters on foot to as far away as the office at High Marley Hill. The office was once the home of the wealthy Berkley family. In 1917 Nellie met Syd Davidson at the Wesleyan chapel where she enjoyed singing and they eventually married in 1924.

Marley Hill Colliery had been abandoned in 1815 by The Grand Alliance, but in 1840 John Bowes had a shaft sunk down to the Hutton seam. Over the years many changes took place. In 1941 the Lodge shaft was sunk down to the Brockwell seam and was probably the most famous one of all. By 1953 the colliery was working in the Brockwell and Tilley seams and a tunnel was driven north to link up with Clockburn Drift near Winlaton Mill some three miles away. The last shaft to be sunk was the West shaft quite close to the existing Lodge shaft. Unfortunately, but in keeping with many other coal mines, Marley Hill Pit fell victim to the policy of the Conservative Government of that time and closed in March 1983.

A row of houses was built around 1845 and a shop added in 1860, which was ran by a family named Bean. Thomas Brabban took over the shop around 1882 and remained there until his death in 1922. The houses became known as 'Post Office Row' after the shop became a post office in 1890, it remained so until 1973. The houses were improved around 1910 to accommodate colliery officials, miners then dubbed it 'Gaffers Row'. Hannah Hutchison took over the shop in the mid 1920s. It was the only shop in the vicinity and as well as being a post office it sold almost everything. Custom was assured from the residents of Colliery Houses, High Row, Andrews Houses and of course the pitmen. The shop stood close to the colliery gates and is pictured here on 1 March 1959. Hannah retired in 1965.

A view looking north along Post Office Row during winter. To the left can be seen the Colliery Ambulance Room which stood on the site of the old Wesleyan chapel. Hannah Hutchison's shop is obscured by snow drifts and at the far end of the street can be seen the colliery offices.

54

A group of miners in the 1800s, they are believed to have worked at Marley Hill.

Pony putter Billy Wilkinson who worked at Blackburn Fell Drift, taking an empty tub in-by for a hewer to fill.

A view taken from the screens at Marley Hill Colliery looking east toward Sunniside. The screening of coal simply meant the removal of stones and other foreign bodies. As many people found out in the days of coal fires, a piece of stone once hot enough was a safety hazard. It would fizz and splutter, then fly out of the hearth in all directions causing everyone to leap out of the way. The screens were a continuous conveyor made up of plates of overlapping metal, as they turned the noise was horrendous. Men or boys stood alongside of the conveyor. This cold and dirty job was once carried out by women who were known as 'Picking Bands'. The coal tubs were brought out of the shaft cage, pushed along a rail and rolled over so that the coal slid down a chute and on to the screens. The stones were then picked out of the coal by hand and thrown down a further chute into a railway truck below. Once full, the engine would shunt the trucks so that an empty one was ready for filling.

The steam driven cage winder house in the early 1900s. In 1953 the steam boilers were replaced by electric.

The pit head baths at Marley Hill Colliery were opened in 1954, they were supervised by Tuppy Larmour, real name David Lawrence. He was always called Tuppy although no one knows why. He played the cornet in the colliery band and was acknowledged as one of the region's best. He eventually became much sought after and played for several bands over the years.

Marley Hill Pit donkey man Bart Davison, c. 1920.

The old blacksmith's shop at Marley Hill Colliery.

Norman Ibbetson, the last 'cage smith' at Marley Hill, responsible for renewing the cage ropes. He served his apprenticeship as a blacksmith from 1942-49 and was fully conversant with all jobs requiring the skills of a blacksmith. His father Jack, known as a 'rolleyway man', worked underground as a rope splicer. Norman is pictured at his home in Sunniside in 1996. He was given the anvil he had worked on for so many years when the colliery closed in 1983.

A group of underground pit lads in 1912. Most of them were pony drivers. Some are carrying their only source of lighting, a midgy lamp. Three of the boys have what appear to be whips tucked in their belts.

The boiler house at Marley Hill Colliery in the early 1900s. James McGahon, second from the right, became a prisoner of war in Germany during the First World War.

Marley Hill Pit bank workers, *c.* 1940. Left to right: H. Preston, G. Sadlar, J. Sharp, P. Brown, P. Burridge, G. Pyle, E. Pinkney and squatting, Mr Lucas with Joe Robinson. Joe, a Sunniside man, was deaf and dumb yet overcame his disabilities and always worked for a living.

Harry Preston (1871-1950) of Sandygate, with pony, at Marley Hill Colliery.

Marley Hill Pit canteen manageress, Ida Parker, with John Ord, in 1953. John was a member of the consultative committee who liaised with the manageress to iron out any problems and ensure a good service for the miners. The canteen was a very important part of the miners' working life. It was open twenty-four hours a day and staffed entirely by ladies. Some of the canteen ladies were married to miners, indeed one or two met their husbands through working there. Some of the canteen staff who worked there over the years were, Ma Barron, Annie Bell, Winnie Young, Polly Graham, Meggy Nicholson, Lillian Ibbetson, Mary King, Mary Hogg, Joy Rowell, Kitty Reid, Violet Herries, and Doris Davis.

Undermanager Fred Kendall, left, and colliery manager, H. Burn, right, in 1953. They are standing beside the cage at the top of the old Brockwell shaft.

Marley Hill miners and their families during the Durham 'Big Meeting Day' in the 1920s. The Miners' Union banner changed in design over the years. This one reads from the top: 'Masters give to your servants. That which is just and equal. Knowing that ye also have a master in heaven.' Below that the wording is mainly obscured and therefore unreadable.

The colliery had its own brass band and many of the players were miners. This is the Marley Hill Colliery Band in 1932. It eventually became known as the Marley Hill Silver Prize Band.

Durham Day. The band marches down towards Sunniside. The Marley Hill Miners' Welfare Hall can be seen to the top of the picture. It was officially opened by the Duke and Duchess of York (later to become the King and Queen) on 29 July 1936. Among the men leading the procession are Miners' Lodge Officials: John Lowden, Joe Hodge, Jack Thompson, and Jack Barmer.

The first leader of the band was Neil McAvoy who owned a Drapers shop in Dewhurst Terrace, (where the Off Licence is now). He was a talented musician, and played for the Queens Hall Orchestra at Newcastle. He is reputed to have taught Sir Thomas Beecham to play the violin. Neil was followed as band leader by Mr White, Luke Harper and finally Alec Boyd. Over the years many people played in the band, among them were: Fred and Harry Rockett, Bill Shorten, Sammy Alfreds, Pup Morton, Bill (Lugs) Armstrong, Jossy Gibson, Wes Prinn, Jack Harn, Paddy Reardon, Tuppy Larmour, Tom Waddle, Bill Liddle, Spikey Patterson, Jack Spinks, Bob Chisholm and Angus Newman. As this certificate shows the band was very professional, entering many competitions with great success.

Many miners and members of the community took an interest in first aid. This is the ambulance class of 1914.

An ambulance class of later years. Mr Christopher Caisley, sitting fourth from the left, was also the permanent Ambulance Man at Marley Hill Colliery.

G. Blackmore. E. Pattinson. R. Milburn. J. W. Armstrong. P. Hinds. C. Hogg. (Capt.) C. Routledge. J. Brown. T. Hearne. J. Batey. S. Treglown. G. Walls. (Trainer)
J. Grey. R. Treglown. (Ass. Sec.) G. F. Grey. Sec.) R. W. Berkley, Esq. (Pres.) J. S. Nesbit, Esq. (Vice-Pres.) W. Lawson, (Treas.) J. Treglown. T. Hogg.
G. Chisholm. R. Chisholm. J. Warmsby.

Marley Hill United Associated Football Club, 1908-9.

Marley Hill football team, *c.* 1950.

The Miners' Welfare Hall was used for many things and local people often put on concerts for fund raising purposes. This is the cast of a typical concert in the 1950s. The mandarin holding the fan is Doug Kendall, a colliery blacksmith. He was a talented singer and best remembered for his favourite song *Old Man River*. He appeared on television as well as performing around the clubs. Standing directly behind him is Davy Mudd, who eventually became an overman at Marley Hill Colliery.

The Kendalls were a well known family in both Marley Hill and Sunniside. On the far left is Doug sitting next to his father Bill, a colliery official. On the far right is Bill's brother Ned, sitting next to Tommy Knox, both of whom were colliery overmen.

Girls from the three villages in 1958. Left to right: Polly Vickery, Maureen Mitchell, Margaret Kilkenny (Ratcliffe), Betty Heron and Ann Greener.

A group of Marley Hill men, c. 1950. Back row: Ronnie Shipley, Davey Mudd, Tom Clifton, Billy Morton. Front row: Jimmy Rutherford, Ned Alexander, Bob Foster, Jack Cassidy and Billy Prinn.

The road from Sunniside to Marley Hill in the early 1900s. St Cuthbert's church is on the top of the hill.

Marley Hill vicarage. It was built around 1885.

The first priest was licensed as a minister of the district of Marley Hill on 23 November 1874. The new parish of St Cuthbert's, Marley Hill was formed from portions of the ancient parishes of; Whickham, Tanfield, and Lamesley and included; Marley Hill, Andrews House and Byermoor Collieries, the hamlets of Crookgate, Sunniside, Tinkler Fell and Streetgate as far as Fugar Bar in Ravensworth. It also included part of Fellside all of which were formerly remote portions of Whickham, Lamesley and Tanfield parishes. St Cuthbert's church was built in 1877 and consecrated by the Bishop of Durham on 15 November 1877. Built in Gothic style, it contains 254 sittings. The first vicar was the Revd Samuel White, 23 November 1874 to 1891. He was followed by the Revds W. J. Wingate, 1892-96, W. D. Croudace, 1897-98, John Arbuckle, 1899-1928, F. W. Probert, 1929-58, Gordon Scott, 1959-62, Alan Gales, 1963-94, and to date, Stephen Radley. The last burial in the church grounds took place on 8 October 1971.

The interior of Marley Hill church with the choir. The altar is a simple flat topped wooden table and raised above the level of the church. It contains the cross and other objects of importance. The aumbry is a small cupboard recessed into the north wall of the church near the altar. It holds vessels containing the reserved Sacrament of the Holy Communion. Over-hanging this cupboard is a lamp with a white light which burns continuously to indicate the presence of the Blessed Sacrament. The organ was built by Nicholson of Newcastle around 1870. The lectern is designed as an eagle with outstretched wings. On the screen separating the choir stalls from the main body of the church is the role of honour of those parishioners who lost their lives during the First World War. On the plaque behind the pulpit are recorded the names of those who lost their lives during the Second World War.

A group of parishioners at the gate of St Cuthbert's church. The little lad in the centre, wearing a cap, is Eddie Hayden of Cuthbert Street, an enthusiastic local historian for most of his life. Eddie became President of the Sunniside and District Local History Society in 1996.

The Revd Francis William Probert, vicar of
Marley Hill church from 1929-58, and his
daughters.

The Revd Alan Gales, vicar of Marley Hill
church from 1963-94.

Marley Hill School was built by Isaac Bewley and cost £3,081 to build, the house cost £600, the fence £80, and the furniture £600. At a ceremony presided over by Mr Thomas Brabban, the school was officially opened by Sir Charles Mark Palmer, a Member of Parliament and local industrialist, on the 1 August 1895. In his speech, Sir Charles expressed confidence in the assured future of the coal mining industry saying, 'It would be a very sad spectacle indeed to have the mines round and about here like so many extinct volcanoes and to see that school standing there as a monument of the past.' Unfortunately in less than 100 years those mines would be extinct. This is the oldest known photograph of the school with the contractors standing in front.

The first headmaster, Mr Lawrence Dewhurst with his wife Miriam and their children, Agnes, William, Charles, Sarah, Lawrence, Janet and Miriam. They moved to Marley Hill from Blackburn in 1884 to live at Sandygate, eventually settling into the school house in 1896. On his retirement they moved to a house named 'San Souci' which means 'Care Free' on Metal Bank at Sunniside. He died in 1926 and is buried in St Cuthbert's church yard. (ABOUT 1895)

Sandygate, Marley Hill, near St Cuthbert's church on the Pit Road, the former home of Mr Dewhurst and his family.

Marley Hill School, at the turn of the century, looking east. Over the years many changes have taken place. In 1964 the school building was updated. This involved adding a hall, kitchen, an extra classroom, and indoor toilets. In 1974 a further classroom was added and in 1978 gas central heating replaced solid fuel. In 1995 the school celebrated its centenary and involved the entire community. The teaching staff led by Adele Evitt and ably assisted by Joan Telford (who has written the history of the school) presided over a first class public relations exercise. The events organised took many weeks of planning and they included a barbecue and fete where the children dressed in costumes of the 1800s. The highlight was probably the concert acted out by the children and based on the diary of Eddie Liddle (who is featured on p.47). Guests of honour were the late Mr Liddle's son, Eddie and his wife Wendy. They had travelled from Midhurst in West Sussex to attend the centenary celebrations. In a supporting roll, the excellent band of Whickham Comprehensive School played at each performance.

Headmaster Lawrence Dewhurst with the school football team of 1912.

Mr Dewhurst with a school class in the early 1900s.

An infants class in the 1920s. Their dress reflecting the dreadful poverty of the working class in those times.

A school football team, 1926-27, with Mr Harry Roddam, Mr Wm Bellerby and Mr John Atkinson.

A class with Miss Weston, *c.* 1926. On the left of the rear row is Mary Harrison who was born 8 March 1913 and is now aged 84 years. Mary wrote an account of her personal memories of Old Sunniside in her younger days for the History Society.

A class with Miss Doreen Nicholson in the 1940s.

A class with Mr Frank Gillender in the late 1940s.

The school football team with Mr Gillender, *c.* 1950.

Marley Hill School viewed from the north in 1938. The railings of the old house curiously named 'Milk & Bread' can be seen to the right.

Bowman's farm to the north of the school. The children of Marley Hill made regular trips across the fields to buy milk and eggs for their families.

Then let us pass our lives in peace
The little time we stay.
Nor let our acts of Friendship Cease
Till life shall pass away.

The last banner of the Marley Hill Mine Workers' Lodge.

Three

Sunniside and Streetgate

The name Sunniside originates from 'Sunnandun' which means the 'Hill of Sunna' and his sons. Sunna was a Saxon tribal chief. Gellesfield originates from Field of Gell (Scandanavian), William and Gilbert (Gilly) Gategang of Gateshead owned the land in 1287. It was known as, Gilbert (or Gilly's) Medowe (Field) which became Gill/Gell's Field. Later, a family called the Claxton's of Old Park, held this meadow for several generations, from 1403-1576. Then, in 1576, Robert Claxton conveyed four acres of Gilbert Medowes (Gellesfield), to William Jennison, Alderman of Newcastle upon Tyne.

The earliest mention of Sunniside, or Gellesfield, sometimes called Gellesriding; appears around the latter part of the sixteenth century. It is recorded that, in 1570, Bishop Pilkington leased to Bartram Anderson (merchant) of Newcastle, the coal mines within Cross Moor in Whickham adjoining the Whaggs, and Newfield on the north, and Gellesfield and Grenleyfield south. Cross Moor west, Gellesfield and Grenleyfield to the south and the road from Newcastle to Street Yate east. These pits with a rent of £30, were only to be open for twenty-one years.

Gellesfield is included in a settlement of the Gibside estates. When on the 26 September 1578, William Blaxton (Blakiston) Esq leased to Cuthbert Hunter (Newcastle) all his coal pits and mines in Gellesfield, with a convenient way through the said field to the water of Darwin (Derwent).

In 1607 William and Ralph Blakiston of Gibside, settled half the close of Gellesfield, and half the mines, to Nicholas Blakiston (second son of William Blakiston), on his marriage to Jane Porter of Shielraws (Shield Row). On the 3 June 1645 Sir Ralph Blakiston (Bart), granted a fourth of Gellesfield Colliery to his brother John Blakiston (Gent). Gellesfield afterwards became the estate of the Brignall family. In a will, dated 20 October 1685, Thomas Brignall of Gellesfield devised, in various proportions, the estate to his wife Florence and his grandchildren, John and Brignell Grainge (Grange) and Isabel and Elizabeth Hall. The grandson, Brignall Grange died in 1701, and left a son, Henry Grange, who married Anne, daughter and co-heir of Francis Middleton of Seaton (Co. Durham). Henry Grange, who died in 1781, left a son, named Middleton Grange (Gent), who became the new owner of the Outhouses and lands of Gellesfield, which was a parcel of the lands of Sunniside. This land called Gellesfield/Galesfield extended from the Whaggs, (waggon-ways), to Sunniside, where there were numerous coal pits in the area, and many of these old cole-ways can be traced, such as, for example, the one that started from Whagg-Gate to Whickham via Whaggs Lane. Waggon-ways were used to bring coals from the pits to the staithes at Derwenthaugh/Swalwell and Dunston, one started at Tanfield and passed through Old Sunniside.

The British Legion Hut was built in 1921 and was officially opened by the Revd John Arbuckle in September of that year. It was made principally of corrugated sheets and stood on land (donated by the Earl of Strathmore) at the west end of the Crescent, opposite the end of Kindreds Wood. Both the Marley Hill and Sunniside Branches of the Legion were responsible for the running of the hut. It was also used for social functions, dances, whist drives, etc. John Aimers was the caretaker in the early 1920s.

The membership of the British Legion was over one hundred strong. These men, outside of the hut, were members in the early 1900s.

Lady members of the British Legion in the early 1900s. Each Remembrance Day a parade, led by the British Legion banner, marched from Sunniside to Marley Hill church. Sadly by the end of the 1950s interest had faded and the Sunniside and Marley Hill Branches of the Legion disbanded.

The Sunniside and Marley Hill members of the Women's Institute, c. 1950.

Old Sunniside overlooked the Black Burn to the north of the Sunniside to Marley Hill road. At its western end stood Old Sunniside farm, more commonly known as 'Tates Farm'. The seventeenth century farmhouse was by far the oldest building in the area, the houses appeared in the early 1800s. The lane, now known as Kingsway, ran from Sunniside Road and past the front of the houses up to the farm. On the other side of the road, running down towards the Black Burn, were the allotments. The houses of Old Sunniside were condemned in 1935 and by December 1936 they were demolished.

Mrs Hannah Buglass at 'The Cottage', Old Sunniside. She originated from Spennymoor and was married to Jack Buglass of Newcastle. After the demolition of Old Sunniside they moved to No. 33, Kingsway.

The daughters of Hannah and Jack, *c.* 1914. Violet is standing, with Mary in her arms, Hetty is on the left and Nelly on the right. In 1993 Mary wrote of her childhood memories at Old Sunniside: 'The layout consisted of 9 houses, then 'Prospect House' with its walled garden. There was also a cottage. The houses were surrounded by gardens, they could be seen very clearly from the main road where the Potter's Wheel is now. I still hold many happy memories of the old village. Old Sunniside farm was occupied by Jack and Mary Anne Routledge in those days, I often went 'tatie' picking for them. I can clearly remember calling at their back door for a can of milk, still warm from the cow. Most houses consisted of one bedroom and a living room with a long scullery (known as the backend), the bedroom was reached by a long ladder, the bedsteads were iron with brass knobs, some had a quilt. If it was cold, a hot brick or an oven shelf in the bed helped and father's top coat made a cosy cover. There was one cold water tap and the house was lit by gas, a penny in the slot. The floors were flagged and covered with lino and proggy mats, they had very little furniture. The large black iron fireplace had a big oven, the fire held about six pailful of coal at a time. Each evening I had the job of filling my father's carbon pit lamp, I also filled his 'baccy' tin and pipe. My mother made ginger beer which was really delicious, she sold this and bunches of mint. Old Sunniside was a very friendly, happy place to live, everyone knew each others business.'

Mrs Jessie Harrison of Prospect House, Old Sunniside. She was married to John Harrison and they had five children, Bill, Andrew, Harry, Maimi, and Matt (who married Mary Buglass of No. 6, Old Sunniside on 4 June 1937). Mrs Harrison died in 1949.

Kingsway looking east in 1938, viewed from inside the Old Sunniside farmyard gates. The council housing which replaced Old Sunniside can be seen on the left. The road ended at those gates, but a lane continued around past the farm and above the top end of Fernville Avenue, travelling across to the Woodman's Arms on Fellside Road. One fields-width above that lane, a track ran from the Crescent on the Sunniside to Marley Hill road across to Bowman's farm, it also led eventually to the Woodman's Arms and on to Fellside Road.

The Chapel Choir at Old Sunniside farm, c. 1930.

The rear of Fernville Avenue in the 1950s, at this time the northern limit of Sunniside. In March 1968 a £3-4 million contract was awarded to Carlton Contractors Ltd to erect 216 houses and 173 garages from the site of Old Sunniside to the fields at the rear of Fernville Avenue. The work commenced in March 1968 and took over a year to complete. The rents were fixed at £4 9s 9d for two bedrooms, £4 17s 10d for three bedrooms and £5 4s 5d for four bedrooms.

The front street of Sunniside looking east in the early 1900s. The old Methodist chapel, built in 1837 (which in 1952 became the Over 60s Hall), is obscured by trees on the right. On the left, at the end of Dewhurst Terrace, can be seen a field. Sun Street was eventually extended on to that land.

The new United Methodist chapel, built by William Hockey of Whickham on a site leased from Lord Ravensworth. It cost £1,200 to build and was opened on 20 August 1910.

The Chapel Choir in the chapel grounds, *c*. 1930.

The ladies attending the opening of the Chapel Hall in 1932, built by Shield Brothers of Swalwell. The 'fox fur', the fashion of the day, is very much in evidence.

The dignitaries present at the opening of the Hall in 1932.

The Methodist Chapel Hall was used for many functions. Over the years local groups formed into concert parties and put on evenings of light entertainment. One local man, Jackie Pearson, sang there on many occasions and often acted as Master of Ceremonies during concerts. He went on to become the concert secretary at Sunniside Club. From the 1930s and up until the early 1950s (before television reached the home), the concerts were thoroughly enjoyed by the local people who used to fill the hall. This photograph is typical of the type of concerts performed.

A group 'dressed up' ready for the carnival in 1930. The little girl, kneeling in the centre, is Betty Shorten, her father Bill led the procession. Standing behind her and wearing a sash with stars on it, is Percy Hutchison. He appeared in many pantomimes, always as the 'dame', and was one of the more extrovert village personalities. On the far left is Dick Clark, the undertaker. The first carnivals were held in a field adjoining Jobling's farm. In later years they moved to Marley Hill football field.

The Bright Sparks Concert Party was formed in 1988 with the intention of raising money for charity. To date they have raised thousands of pounds for charities such as, The Marie Curie Institute, McMillan Nurses, Motor Neuron Disease and Multiple Sclerosis. They make their own costumes and travel many miles to entertain people all over the region. They are pictured here with the Mayor and Mayoress of Gateshead, Mr and Mrs Henderson. Standing, left to right: Joan Heron, Davy Mudd, Edna Brown, the Mayor and Mayoress, Ruth Soulsby, Tess Larmour and George Bright. Sitting: Betty Williams, Fred Rockett, Nell Armstrong, Nancy Mudd, Ted Young, and in front, Phyllis Tulip.

The original Bright Sparks. Sadly some have passed away but the group have the attitude, 'The show must go on'. They continue to perform and help those less fortunate than themselves. Back row, left to right: Kathy Caisley, Davey Mudd, Tess Larmour, Ruth Soulsby, Joan Heron, Phyliss Tulip, Edna Brown, Tuppy Larmour. Front row, left to right: Betty Williams, Freddy Rockett, Nell Armstrong, Nancy Mudd, Ted Young.

The Sunniside Branch of Burnopfield Co-op was opened at Nos 1 and 2, Dewhurst Terrace by the President of the Society, Mr J.W. Bell in July 1911. There were grocery, butchery and drapery departments with leisure facilities upstairs. In 1921 new premises were opened adjoining the top end of Dewhurst Terrace, Mr Robert Heslop performed the opening ceremony.

The Co-op closed in 1987 and the shop was eventually taken over as a Spa. On Thursday 12 March 1992 at approximately 4.30 am a fire started. It was whipped up by gale force winds and the entire building was destroyed. The remaining shell was unsafe and had to be totally demolished. In its place was built a supermarket with shops attached. The supermarket was opened on the 16 September 1993 by Coronation Street star Ken (Reg Holdsworth) Morley.

Lizzy Parkin and Betsy Dinning with children, sitting on the field at the Chapel Opening. The field is now the site of Sun Hill sheltered accommodation which was built in 1968 by George Wimpey at a cost of £80,000.

Bob Dinning, the son of Betsy, worked at Marley Hill and Watergate Colliery in his younger days. He took an active interest in Sunniside Methodist chapel and was the Sunday School Superintendent for some time. He married Doris Wright and they had a daughter Ann. As a family they contributed greatly to the running of the chapel, giving of their time and effort constantly.

An unknown group at the Chapel Opening. This field was used over the years primarily for football matches, it was also used extensively by local children. There was great concern when the council decided to build on it, but by promising an alternative sports field the council managed to avoid public protest. Unfortunately, the promised field was never to materialise.

This is the oldest known photograph of Sunniside looking west, taken in the late 1800s, when the road was just a dirt track. There are no street lights and to the right, past the Rising Sun on the corner of the Sunniside to Whickham road, can be seen a field in the middle of the village. At the time this picture was taken the woods came right down to where the Co-op store was eventually built at the west end of the village.

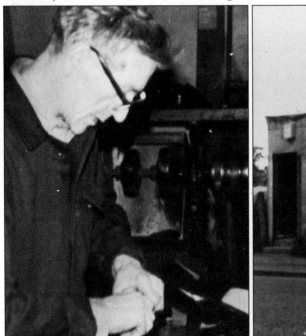

Left: Ernie Boyd, born in 1920, at work in his cobblers shop, opposite the new Methodist chapel at Sunniside. Ernie spent fifty-six years as a cobbler, he retired in November 1986. During his working life Ernie had repaired footwear for generations of families. His more famous customers were Lord Gort of Hamsterley Hall and the great Newcastle United footballer Hughie Gallagher. Right: The 8ft by 10ft cobblers shop, built in sections on the gardens in front of No. 5, Prospect Terrace by Robert Swan Boyd, Ernie's father, and a friend in the 1930s. They then carried it piece by piece and assembled it into position opposite the chapel, it would remain there for sixty-one years. The humble shop provided a modest living for Robert Swan Boyd and his son until they reached retirement age. The shop was demolished in 1993.

Jack Johnston, Joe Croft and Sid Clark outside Reed's butchers shop, next to the Methodist chapel, Sunniside, in the 1930s. Jack worked for Reed from 1920 until his retirement in 1966. Sid worked there from 1928 and Joe served his apprenticeship there, he eventually became the Co-op store butcher. Jack and Joe were arguably the finest leek growers in the area. Men came from far and wide to seek their advice and to buy their leek seeds for the following year's shows.

The Traveller's Rest Inn, Sunniside. The bus is of the type in use around 1925. At that time the landlord was Richard Dillon. He was married to Lottie who at one time ran a fish shop next door to the pub. In the late 1920s Tom Punshon took over and the pub became commonly known as 'Punshon's'. Marley Hill Colliery Band practiced in the back room every Sunday for many years.

The Rising Sun Inn (formerly the Sun Inn), built in the mid 1800s. Some of the licensees over the years have been, William Wilson in 1841, William Rutherford in 1850, William Surtees in 1856, Dorothy Storey in 1861, Robert Storey in 1873, James Davison in 1878, Joseph Davison in 1907, Jimmy Davison in 1934, Arthur and Doris Scorer, 1955 until 1983.

The eight daughters of Robert and Dorothy Storey residing at the Sun Inn in 1861. Robert worked at Marley Hill Colliery. Dorothy ran the pub, helped by her daughters.

Left: Sunniside looking west in the 1940s, with the Methodist chapel on the right. Right: Lottie Brabban (nee Rutherford) with her husband Billy. She was a very popular hard working person. She was the caretaker of the White Elephant School at Streetgate in the 1930s and also worked in the fields for local farmers. Lottie could often be seen wearing a man's flat cap and could work as hard as a man. During the First World War she worked in Marley Hill cokeworks while the men were away fighting. Billy died in 1932 and Lottie in the early 1950s.

Lottie and Billy Brabban at their white washed cottage which stood next to the White Elephant School at Streetgate and opposite Jobling's farm. The cottage had two rooms with stone floors and was once occupied by a local blacksmith. It was demolished in the early part of 1960. Police housing replaced it.

Hannah Elizabeth (1861-1940) and Charles Thacker Shorten (born 1868) were brother and sister and were born in Norfolk. In 1874, along with their parents Richard and Sarah and their brothers and sisters, they walked from Norfolk to the North East to seek work. As a Coldstream Guard, Richard had fought in the Crimean War in 1854 and had suffered terribly with frostbite. He was nursed back to health by Florence Nightingale (The Lady With The Lamp). His brother Charles, his wife Martha and their children also made the trek. Richard's family settled at Fugar Bar and Charles' at Colliery Houses, Old Marley Hill, then at Langley Park. Hannah's mother died at an early age so she devoted her life to bringing up the family and never married. Her younger brother Charles remained a bachelor and lived with Hannah until her death.

John Robert Shorten (1875-1941), the son of Richard and Sarah, was the first of the family to be born in the region. He married Margaret Shearlaw (1876-1954) on 14 August 1897. She originated from Edinburgh and worked as a maid at Swan's farm, Streetgate. John and Margaret are pictured here with two of their children, Richard William (1898-1982) and Violet (1899 - c. 1986). They lived at No. 9, Prospect Terrace, Sunniside. Margaret became invaluable to the village. She acted as a midwife, also tending the sick and dying at all hours of the day and night.

Jim Shorten (1879-1967) with his wife Anne (1879-1968). Jim was the second son of Richard and Sarah to be born in the region. He and Anne are best known for having run a fish shop in Dewhurst Terrace, Sunniside for many years.

Left: Albert Joseph Shorten (1900-1966), son of John and Margaret. He became a miner at Marley Hill. Right: Margaret MacIntyre (Peggy) Shorten, daughter of John and Margaret. She married Jack Ledger and moved to Dipton.

Left: Adam James Shorten, son of John and Margaret. He became a miner at Marley Hill and then emigrated to Australia with his family. His widowed sister, Violet and her children Ruby and Clive, joined him in Australia 1959. Right: Alice Clarke Shorten (1914-78), youngest daughter of John and Margaret. She married Fred Newman and lived at No. 6, Prospect Terrace. The Shorten family were one of the largest families ever to occupy a two room house at Prospect Terrace.

The back lane of Prospect Terrace was of rough gravel, backing on to market gardens. The refuse bins were placed at the back doors and the women hung their washing out across the lane. The binmen would drive up the length of the terrace and often had to lift washing out of their way.

The front of Prospect Terrace looking down on to Sunniside Road. Built in the 1850s, the ten houses were little better than a slum. Each house consisted of one bedroom, a stone floored living room and a tiny back kitchen with one cold water tap. The toilets were in a field at the top of the street, one shared between two houses. At the bottom of the terrace was a small room, this was used by the Home Guard during the Second World War and by Bobby Lowdon as a storeroom in later years. The terrace was demolished in 1960 and was used in the construction of bus shelters around the area.

Two children at the front of the Terrace was once used for growing produce, but in the late 1930s, the gardens which ran down to the Black Lonnen became overgrown. During the Second World War Anderson shelters were dug into position within yards of the front path.

Hole Lane looking east toward the junction of Sunniside Road, *c.* 1910. The name derives from Gellesfield Hole, where there was once a colliery. The lane forms the border between Marley Hill and Whickham Parish.

Metal Bank on Sunniside Road, *c.* 1910. In the eighteenth century coal trucks passed down here to join up with Dunston Waggonway. The curious name is thought to have been given in the early 1900s because of the hard flint like chippings used as a covering.

Sunniside Social Club, pictured here in the 1920s with Club Steward Jack Creitch, was formed in 1914. The founder members took over Rose Cottage, a small building which stood on the edge of the lane. In 1918 a new club was built very close to Rose Cottage, it was small but with improved facilities. The club struggled financially during the years of the First World War and throughout the depression of the 1920s. On 20 August 1919 Mr Robert Brabban gave a £30 loan to the club to help it survive. By the end of the Second World War the building was in a deplorable state, the roof was leaking, the floor was rotten and the club was in debt. The men came back from their military service and set to work to repair the club. Its trading position improved and Rose Cottage was demolished in the late 1950s to allow the club to expand. Many changes have taken place over the years and the club has played a very important part in the social life of the village for generations of people.

The success of Sunniside Club is due to the work so freely given by enthusiasts who have served on club committees. Probably the most influential person in the history of the club was Victor Dillon. He went on to become the Chairman of the Board of Directors at The Federation Brewery. This was the club committee around 1974: Back row: John Poulton, Billy Arnold, Tom Heron, Harold Atkinson, Eddie Pack. Middle Row: Tom Bell, Arthur Crossling, Angus Newman, Peter Graham, Ray Cranney. Front row: Fred Newman (Treasurer), Billy Liddle (Secretary and now a Director at the Federation Brewery), Victor Dillon (Chairman), Jean & Alan Gleghorn (Steward & Stewardess) and Arnold Reid.

Two very well known former club members playing a hand of dominoes; John Lowden, Marley Hill Miners Lodge Official, and Jack Thompson, a Lodge Official and a Local Councillor.

The club had table service for many years and lots of local ladies found part time employment at the club. Alma Newman, on the left, and Audrey Newman, in the centre, (pictured here with their sister Alie) were waitresses for many years. Others who served in the past were Joan Heron, Lizzie Wheatley, Stella Churnside, May Cutter, Mavis Debie, Susan Heron, Sylvia Bell, Magdalen Graham, Audrey Taskas, Audrey Knight, Mary Lowden, Margaret Lowden, Iris Skelton, Jean Wallace, Michele Dickinson and many more.

The club interior is beautifully decorated and furnished. It is very comfortable and boasts many amenities. Its close relationship with the Northern Clubs Federation Brewery has been of mutual benefit, with low prices, excellent products and a barrelage dividend. Pictured here is a History Society Christmas party. Sitting at the top of the room facing the camera is Sheila Gascoigne (Treasurer), on the left, and Eleanor Baty (Secretary).

The White Elephant School, viewed from the south, was destroyed by fire on 7 March 1975. The original building was erected in 1914, although it did not become an Infants School until 1923. During its lifetime there were only three headteachers, Miss Hannah Armstrong 1923-48, Miss Lesley Cuthbert 1948-51 and Miss Mabel Davison 1951-62. Mrs A. Grant was acting head until the school's closure in 1963. Over the years, other teachers were, Elizabeth Morgan, Ethel Sample, Jean Lamb, Mrs Binks, Jean Dawson and Mrs C. Doran. Following its closure, it was bought by Dumighan Brothers. They sold it to Mr McLennan a heating engineer who used it as a warehouse until it caught fire. No one knows the true origin of the name White Elephant.

The remains of the White Elephant School following the fire. The site was bought by Harry Brown in 1984, who cleared it and had a bungalow built there. He named it 'High Trees'.

A class at the White Elephant School in 1927. Florence Clark (Wilson), the owner of the photograph, is standing fifth from the left.

A class of 1951-52 with Miss Jean Dawson.

Streetgate looking down toward the Rose Shamrock & Thistle, *c.* 1910. The name is thought to derive from the location of the waggonway running down to the staithes. At that point it ran straight through the gates at Pennyfine and down Bakers Bank, combining 'straight and gate', eventually becoming Streetgate.

The original Rose Cottage at Streetgate owned by Mr and Mrs Young (pictured). Rose Cottage in its present form bear's little resemblance to the original. The present owner is Betty Burness.

The wheelwright, Thomas Liddle (1766-1849) and his children. His shop was near the Rose Shamrock & Thistle.

The Toll Cottage near Fugar Bar was operated as such until the toll was discontinued around 1878, the road at that time was known as Turnpike Road. It stood on the east side of the bridge which crossed the waggonway. Mary Sinclair was the keeper in 1841. Elizabeth Annie Stott lived there after she retired as landlady at the Rose Shamrock & Thistle in the early part of the 1900s. The Toll Cottage was demolished around 1938.

The Rose Shamrock & Thistle during the tenancy of Elizabeth Ann Stott, *c*. 1902. First of all named Union Inn, Robert Stott renamed it 'The Rose & Thistle' in the late nineteenth century. His son Billy took over the tenancy and promptly renamed it 'The Rose Shamrock & Thistle'. By 1902 Billy's wife Elizabeth Ann had taken over, presumably following her husband's death. After Elizabeth retired, Thomas Storey took over and made structural changes. The name remained the same, however, until the late 1980s when it was renamed 'The Rose'.

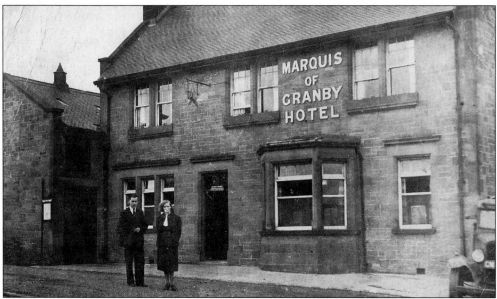

Arthur and Doris Scorer, the tenants of the Marquis of Granby, *c*. 1938. The building was first used as a pub in the early 1800s and was named after the original Marquis who was born in 1721 and died in 1770. The first tenant was Margaret Pyle in 1861, followed by William (Bill of the Bank) Laidman. It was during his tenancy that the infamous murder of Joseph Leybourne took place in August 1865. There have been many tenants over the years, the Scorer's took over in February 1938. It is said that during their tenancy the ghost of Leybourne first appeared. They stayed at the Marquis for eighteen years before moving to the Rising Sun at Sunniside in 1955.

Left: Billy and Elizabeth Anne Stott, former tenants of the Rose Shamrock & Thistle, c. 1900. Right: The blacksmith's shop at Pennyfine, with John, Bob and George Wallace. The Wallace family took over the forge in the early 1800s, at first living in the cottage which would eventually belong to Lottie Brabban. John was born in 1876 and worked until he was 80 years of age. His son George took over in 1956, but there became less need for a blacksmith as modern machinery took over the role of the carthorse and travelling by car replaced the horse. To earn a living George became a milkman until his retirement in 1983 and the forge eventually closed.

The family of Richard Shorten, c. 1914. Standing, left to right: Leo, Edith, Richard, James and Alfred. Seated: Richard, Eleanor (Nellie) and Charlotte. The family came from Norfolk and settled at Streetgate and their first son James was born there in 1875. James, his wife Edith and their children eventually emigrated to America. In July 1994, the grand-daughter of James and Edith, Marjorie Keen (who lives at Parkesburg Pennsylvania), brought her grand-daughter Megan over to England to trace their ancestry. Marjorie very kindly donated this photograph.

Ravensworth Cottage, Coach Road, 31 July 1913.

Ravensworth Castle stood to the north west of Lamesley. The castle occupied the site of an old fortress called Ravenshelm and two of its towers were embodied in the new building. It is possible, given the origin of the name, that the invading Danes built the first fortress. The castle became the ancestral home of the Liddells, the first of whom was Thomas, who acquired the manor and castle of Ravenshelm in the late 1500s. After a long line of Liddells, Sir Thomas Henry Liddell succeeded in 1791. In 1808 he had Ravenshelm rebuilt and redesigned by the architect John Nash. The sixth Baron of Ravensworth, Gerald Wellesley, sold off the castle's treasures in 1920 and left the area to live at Alnwick. The castle then became a residential school for girls from 1921 until 1926. Then because of mineworkings under the castle it began to subside and break up. The seventh Lord Ravensworth, Robert Arthur Liddell, succeeded in 1932 but he never lived in the castle. He died on 4 August 1950 and the castle was eventually demolished.

The Ravensworth estate male employees at a social gathering, *c.* 1895.

The Ravensworth estate female employees at the same gathering, *c.* 1895.

The woods on the Ravensworth Estate were a haven for wildlife and had many varied species of trees and plants, especially rhododendrons. It was a very popular area for walks, always culminating in a visit to the beautiful castle grounds. These young men in the early 1900s, like generations before them, are enjoying a visit to Ravensworth.

In 1868 William Brabban was the tenant of the farm at Loosing Hill (now commonly known as 'Joblings'). This cart was in use during his tenancy.

A member of the Brabban family at their farm.

Sunniside Associated Football Club, 1913-14.

Sunniside A.F.C., *c.* 1945.

Sunniside Imperials football team with their trainers and other officials, *c.* 1950.

Sunniside Imps, *c.* 1950. From right to left: Tom Heads, Elgy Charlton, John Greener, -?-, Jim Eltringham, Mervyn Nelson, Joe Porter, -?-, George Spraggon, -?-, Danny Tinnion.

Ravensworth Shop Colliery was situated approximately three miles east of Sunniside. Like every other mine in the area it is long gone.

Bakers Bank Head control box at Pennyfine. Left to right: C. Henderson, N. Christer, Eli Watson and N. Callon. The level crossing on Pennyfine Road was operated from this box.

An engine bringing full coal trucks down to Bakers Bank Head ready for their journey by gravity haulage to Dunston Staithes.

The full trucks were attached to a cable at the top of the bank. The cable ran around a huge wheel under the rails and down to Watergate. A set of empty trucks were attached to the cable at that end and once the brakesman at Bakers Bank Head allowed the wheel to turn, the full trucks rolled off down the bank, their weight pulled the empty ones up, passing each other en-route. A bankrider sat on each set. Their job was to free the cable once the set reached its destination.

It is fitting that we end our journey through the three villages at Dunston Staithes which has played such a vital role in our coal mining industry. Many have heard of the staithes, but even though millions of tons of our coal were transported from there, few know anything of its history. Dunston born Ethel Baker is greatly interested in the staithes and has carried out a detailed research of the subject: The staithes were built by the North Eastern Railways, the first pile was driven on 26 August 1890. There was no formal ceremony when it opened on Monday 16 October 1893. The first steamship loaded was called *The Holmside*. The staithes is a timber structure made from North American pitch pine, the total weight of timber used was 3,200 tons. It is 526 metres long with four railway tracks leading to six loading berths (three on each side). There are two loading chutes to each berth. The cost was huge, especially in those days, the final total being £210,000. The staithes created employment for dozens of men, some of them, the trimmers and teamers, were very high earners, earning as much as £10 per week in 1930. It was a dirty, noisy and dangerous place to work and during the night the men worked in candlelight until electricity arrived in 1930. The winter months were particularly harsh. The blizzards swept up the river and the coal froze in trucks making life miserable for the men. After just one year coal shipments had increased from 20,000 to 130,000 tons per annum. In 1894 1,289,000 tons were shipped from the staithes in 1,037 vessels. In the late 1920s, 140,000 tons of coal were being shipped weekly, but from the end of the Second World War trade steadily declined. The run down was gradual and it closed as a working staithes in 1977, closing finally in 1980. The role it had played was recognised when it was restored to be part of our national industrial heritage and declared a Grade A listed building.

Four
Those Who Served

It is with great pride that we devote this section to those who have served in the Armed Forces. Our small villages produced many Servicemen who fought valiantly throughout two World Wars and in military campaigns of a lesser degree since then. Many fell in battle and never returned home, some returned but were broken in body and spirit. The families of those men suffered too, not only the dreadful sense of loss but many years of extreme hardship. We pay tribute to them and to the other brave people in uniform who continually serve us so well, especially our Police Officers and our Fire Fighters.

Robert Dickson. A soldier from the Hobson who served in the First World War.

Left: William Kilkenny who served in the First World War. He contracted malaria during his service which contributed to his death around 1932. Right: Two soldiers during the First World War from the Vickery family.

Bill Shorten of Sunniside and his life long friend Norman Nicholson of Marley Hill. They both served in the Royal Artillery during the First World War and fought in the Somme. They are pictured here with Florence Nicholson, on the left, and Alice Nicholson, on the right. The lady in the centre is unknown.

A Regiment of Royal Engineers during the First World War bringing sandbags forward. Among those in the foreground is Thomas Colledge who was invalided out when mustard gas destroyed his lungs.

Thomas and Agnes Reay during the First World War with their son Robert. It was possibly the last time that little Robert saw his father. Thomas was killed in action when Robert was only three years of age.

John and Ina Todd during the First World War.

In Affectionate and Loving Remembrance of

Lance Corpl. James Shearlaw,

Cameron Highlanders,

Killed in action, Somewhere in France,

October 18th, 1916.

Aged 25 years.

———

Dearly beloved brother of Mrs. J. R. Shorten.

Prospect Terrace,
Sunniside,
Gateshead.

" And God shall wipe all tears away, and there shall be no more death."

Deeply lamented and sadly mourned by his only Sister.

During the slaughter of the First World War many hundreds of soldiers were killed and their remains never found. Memorial cards were the only way some relatives could express their grief. Jim Shearlaw of the 5th Battalion, The Cameron Highlanders was killed. In the absence of his remains, and therefore no grave, his name was carved on Pier 15, Face B of the Thiepval War Memorial in France. His sister Margaret had the memorial card produced.

The First World War memorial erected at the Causey. Nine men were killed from that tiny and close knit community, a very heavy price to pay.

James McGahon (born 25 November 1892, died 24 December 1979) pictured during his service with the Drake Battalion, British Expeditionary Force in the First World War.

(If replying, please quote the sailor's Name and Official No.)

RECORD OFFICE, 63rd (ROYAL NAVAL) DIVISION,

B/MM

47, Victoria Street,

London, S.W. 1.

18th June, 1917.

Sir,

I regret to have to inform you that a report has been received from the War Office to the effect that your Son, Leading Seaman James McGahon, Tyneside, Z/2067, Howe Battalion, was admitted to the 18th General Hospital, Dannes Camiers, on the 9th June, 1917, suffering from severe gun-shot wound of the right Thigh and Face. was wounded in action while serving with the B.E.F.,

on the ___

I am at the same time to express the sympathy and regret of this Department.

Any further information received in this office as to his condition will be at once notified to you.

I am,

Your obedient Servant,

Simpson

Lieut. Colonel.

O. in C. Records, 63rd (R.N.) Division.

Mr. M. McGahon,
46, Middle Row,
Marley Hill,
DURHAM.

5000/12/16=[682] 9017/P994 5000 5/17 T925 G & S 110

During the war Jimmy was wounded and his family at Middle Row, Colliery Houses, Marley Hill received this letter. On 16 May 1918 the family received a letter stating that Jimmy was missing. Fortunately he had been taken prisoner and put to work in a coal mine in Germany. He tried to escape but was destined to remain a prisoner until the end of the war. On his return home Jimmy received a letter from the King welcoming him back.

Members of the Durham Light Infantry during the First World War. On the left of the back row is Robert W. Brabban who was wounded in the abdomen during the battle for 'Hill 60' in France.

Arthur Dixon Scorer of the Durham Light Infantry during the Second World War. At the time of his conscription, he was the licensee of the Marquis of Granby public house at Fugar Bar. His wife Doris ran the pub during his absence throughout the war years. He took part in the D. Day landings and received superficial shrapnel wounds which necessitated a period of hospitalisation.

F.G. Newman (snr) joined the Northumberland Fusiliers during the Second World War. He took part in the Italian campaign at Monte Casino and then the North African campaign. His civilian trade had been as a chef and because of that he was eventually transferred to the Catering Corp. He is seen here wearing a beret and standing next to the man in the white vest.

Right: Letters home were subject to censorship. Usually the troops were issued with a standard note designed to let the families know that they were at least alive. This rather irreverent military Christmas card was typical of the notelets issued.

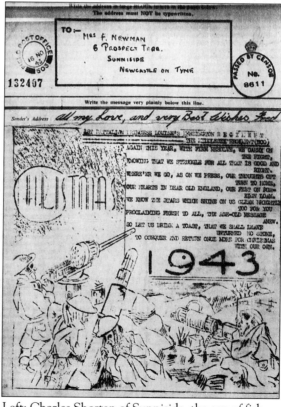

Left: Charles Shorten of Sunniside, the son of fish shop owners Jim and Anne. He served during the Second World War.

Andrew Graham (Merchant Navy) pictured at his marriage to Magdalen Kilkenny on 12 May 1943. He served as a gunner on the Russian convoys during the Second World War when they were continually attacked by German U. Boats and the Luftwaffe. He was also involved in the Spanish Civil War.

Douglas Dickinson during his service in the Second World War with the Gordon Highlanders. He was based at Palestine in the Middle East.

The Home Guard were the butt of many jokes when in reality they did an excellent job. They assisted in rescue work and casualty evacuation as well as helping to enforce the blackout. In some instances they actually shot down enemy aircraft and spent many cold nights in observation posts. Shown here is the Marley Hill Home Guard: Back Row: Joe Simpson, Tommy Simpson, Billy Eddy, Fred Johnson, Jimmy Cook, -?-, Tommy Clifton. Front Row: Bob Forster, Joe Bell, Billy Young, Billy Dent, Scamp, Tom Davidson, Alf Nelson.

Right: F.G. Newman of Sunniside served in the Royal Marines, 1959-68. With 40 Commando in Malta, 1961-62 and with 41 Commando in Devon 1962-63. In 1964, with 45 Commando, he fought in Aden near the Yemen border during the Radfan and Southern Arabia campaigns. For a short period he was attached to the 2nd Parachute Regiment at Bahrain, he temporarily joined the 3rd Commando Brigade in Singapore. On 23 January 1964, by then an N.C.O, he took part in the first ship to shore helicopter assault ever launched by British Marines. Following a plea to the British Government by President Julius Nyrere of Tanganyika East Africa, 45 Commando sailed from Aden and launched a successful attack, from the Aircraft Carrier H.M.S. *Centaur*, against rebel troops. He ended his service career as an instructor at the Commando Training Centre in Devon and at the R.M. Depot Deal in Kent.

D. Young of Byermoor served in the Royal Navy from 1957-66. He was a crew member of the famous aircraft carrier *The Ark Royal*.

Left: P. Kelly, originally from Manchester, served in the Royal Marines from 1959-69. He joined 40 Commando in Malta, 1961-62. On his return to England he met and married Alma Newman of Sunniside. He was based at 43 Commando in Plymouth in 1962-63. In 1964 he joined 45 Commando in Aden and fought in the Radfan and Southern Arabian campaigns. His last tour of duty abroad was with the 3rd Commando Brigade based in Singapore, during that time he served in Malaya and Hong Kong. He ended his service career at Eastney Barracks, Portsmouth.

R.A. Graham, born at Byermoor, served in the Royal Army Medical Corp from 1963-73. During his service he was posted to British Guiana, Singapore, Malaya, Borneo and Cyprus.

The campaign medals of three generations in one family; Crimean War, Second World War and Aden.

On Saturday 20 March 1993, at approximately 11.00 pm, Police Sergeant William Forth and P.C. William Hay were called to deal with an incident on Clover Hill at Sunniside. That night, in a shameful and cowardly attack, Sergeant William Forth was brutally murdered. On 24 March 1995 the front street of Sunniside came to a halt for the unveiling of a memorial in honour of William Forth. Pictured here, during the ceremony, are left to right: Michael Winner, Chairman of the Police Memorial Fund, Tony Blair the leader of the Labour Party, Sergeant Forth's son and his widow Gill. Mr Blair (to become Prime Minister in 1997) also laid a wreath on behalf of the then Premier John Major. The police are engaged in a never ending battle and they constantly risk their lives on our behalf. We should be eternally grateful to the officers of the 'thin blue line'.